Salomon Munk

Philosophy and Philosophical Authors of the Jews

A Historical Sketch with Explanatory Notes

Salomon Munk

Philosophy and Philosophical Authors of the Jews
A Historical Sketch with Explanatory Notes

ISBN/EAN: 9783337079727

Printed in Europe, USA, Canada, Australia, Japan

Cover: Foto ©Thomas Meinert / pixelio.de

More available books at **www.hansebooks.com**

PHILOSOPHY

AND

PHILOSOPHICAL

AUTHORS OF THE JEWS.

A HISTORICAL SKETCH

WITH EXPLANATORY NOTES,

BY

S. MUNK,

Librarian of the National Library at Paris (France). Author of many Eminent Scientific Works.

TRANSLATED BY

DR. ISIDOR KALISCH.

CINCINNATI:
BLOCH & CO.'S PRINTING HOUSE,
1881.

PREFACE.

My principal design in publishing this little volume is to give
to the public an English translation of a highly-learned and a
very interesting sketch of the Jewish philosophy as it appeared
in France (Paris, 1849), under the title, " La Philosophie Chez
les Juifs par," S. Munk, Librarian at the Parisian National Library, etc., which is originally contained in the " Dictionaire des
Sciences Philosophiques." It was translated into German, with
additional notes, by Dr. B. Beer. For this portion of philosophy
discussed in the book is still generally a *terra incognita* to many ;
yes, it is like a cemetery, where there are a few epitaphs of some
learned Jews, consisting merely of their names, but their works,
ideas and principles are buried in oblivion. Therefore Professor
Dr. Julius Fuerst very correctly remarks, in his introduction to
his German translation of "Emunoth Wedeoth," preface, page
vi. : " They take haughty leaps in the gradation of history ; although the steps are not wanting. They take no notice of the
many links in the great chain of philosophy of religion which
were wrought by Jews with constant effort in the course of many
centuries."

But the reason of such a negligence of the Jewish philosophy,
especially of the Middle Ages, may be, because the works of
Jewish *literati* at that time were mostly written in the Arabian
and Hebrew languages, which are not understood by laymen,
and which can be read even by professional men with great
difficulty. In the work before us the great Orientalist, S. Munk,
sketched in a masterly manner the endeavors and researches
made by Jewish scholars and their vast movements in the bat-
talion of thoughts in ancient times and in the Middle Ages,
and thus supplied the desideratum felt by every liberal and
honest lover of truth.

May this new book be kindly received in the dominions of
philosophy and religion, is the sincere wish of the translator.

Fasit Deus!

HISTORICAL SKETCH

— OF —

JEWISH AUTHORS OF ANCIENT TIMES

And the Middle Ages in the Domain of Philosophy.

To KNOW God and to make him known to the whole world, was the mission which was alloted to the Jewish people. But they were led to the knowledge of God by suggestions of faith and by a revelation which they received without adding to it anything themselves. The savans and prophets of the ancient Hebrews, appealing to the heart of man, to its moral feeling and to the imagination, endeavored to cherish and promulgate the belief in a unique Being, the Creator of all things.

The Hebrews did not try to penetrate into the secret of the divine Being. The existence of God, the spirituality of the soul, the knowledge of good and evil are not the results of a series of inferences.

They believed in God, the Creator, who revealed himself to their ancestors, and his existence seemed to them to be beyond the arguments of human reason. Their morality flowed naturally from conviction and from the intrinsic feeling of a just and good God. Therefore, there are in all their books no traces of metaphysical speculations, as are to be found in those of the Hindoos and Greeks.

They do not possess a philosophy in the sense of the word as we understand it.

Mosaism in its theological part presents to us neither a scientific theology nor a philosophical system, but merely a religious doctrine, based upon revelation. Many points of this doctrine, however, although they are couched in poetical terms, belong indisputably to the province of philosophy, and we perceive in that the endeavor of human thought to solve certain problems regarding the absolute Being in revelation to man.

The existence of evil in a world which owes its origin to a Being that is the Supreme Goodness awakened especially the reflection of the Hebrew savans.

How is it possible to admit the real existence of evil without prescribing limits to that Being from whom no evil can emanate? And how can we admit such limitations without denying the unity of the Absolute Being and without adopting the doctrine of Dualism?

The evil, says the Mosaic doctrine, has no real existence. It does not exist in the creation at all; because, as the creation proceeded from God, there can not be any place for the evil.

Thus it reads at the close of every period of creation: " And God saw that it was good."

The evil made its appearance in the world just when intelligence came, that is, at the same moment when man, an intellectual, moral being, was destined to grapple with matter. It happened then that a collision of the spiritual with the material principle took place, which produced the evil; because man, endowed with moral feeling and free in his movements, should endeavor to bring all his actions in unison with the supreme good; but when he allows matter to overpower him, the evil is engendered by himself. This doctrine of evil, contained in the third chapter of Genesis, is closely connected with the doctrine of freedom of will, one of the fundamental doctrines of Mosaism.

Man possesses an absolute freedom in using his faculties. Life and good, and death and evil are in his power (Deuter. xxx. 15–19).

It is important to let this doctrine derive its efficacy from this passage.

The Jews have always subordinated to it the manifold philosophical doctrines of foreign origin which they adopted at different periods.

The development of this doctrine in its relations to the divine providence and to the will of God as the only cause of creation, was always considered by the Jewish sages of all times one of the most important subjects of reflection. Maimonides, Moreh Nebuchim, 1, 3, ch. xvii.

The *literati* among the Hebrews and Mohammedans contented themselves with the cultivation of poetry and that practical wisdom which the Orientals like to clothe in the form of parables, proverbs and enigmas.

The religion of the Hebrews granted no room for real philosophical speculations.

In the councils of learned men important philosophical questions were sometimes engendered, but they were treated from a religious standpoint and in a poetical form. Thus. for instance, we find in the book of Job an assembly of wise men trying to solve the problems of divine Providence and of human destiny.

After a long, unsuccessful explanation, God himself appears in a thunder-storm, and accuses man of the audacity in desiring to judge the mysterious ways of Providence. Man can only behold the works of creation with awe and astonishment, when everything in nature is a great secret to him; how, then, could he judge the inscrutable motives of the divine Providence, and the government of the universe? Man is not able to know the ways of the infinite Being. He shall bow down before the Almighty and be resigned to his will. This is the final principle of the book of Job, which has decidedly a purely religious tendency, and allows the human reason too little power to favor the philosophical speculation.

The book of Ecclesiastes arrived nearly at the same conclusion, showing traces of a well-considered skepticism, presupposing certain efforts of the intellect whose insufficiency the author has perceived and alluded to, even (Eccl. xii. 12) to an exuberance of books, wherein the human spirit endeavored to solve problems which are beyond its power. But this very book, which is ascribed to Solomon, shows us by its diction and ideas a period when foreign culture was already exercising an influence with the Hebrews. It was indisputably composed after the Babylonian captivity, and therefore the spiritual condition of the ancient Hebrews can not be inferred from that at all. The Babylonian exile and all the events that followed it brought the Jews in contact with the Chaldeans and Persians, who did not fail to exercise a certain influence upon the civilization and even upon the religious views of the Jews. The influence of the tenets which are contained in Zend-Avesta we perceive already in some books of the Old Testament, especially in Ezekiel, Zachariah and Daniel.

The true worshipers of Jehovah did not manifest that abhorrence to the religious views of the Persians which they showed against those of other heathen nations. The religion of the Zend-Avesta, although she does not teach an absolute monotheism, is, nevertheless, just as hostile to idolatry as the Jewish religion.

The spirituality of the Persian religion was the main cause which induced the Jews in their relations to that people to be less reserved, and many Persian religious views were adopted by them and became national by degrees.

Parseeism, however, contains too little of the speculative elements, that it could of itself not have engendered the philosophical speculation among the Jews.

The prevailing character of the Jewish Scriptures under the Persian King and during the period of the Macedonian government remained essentially the same after as it was before the Babylonian exile; only the frequent intercourse with the Greeks and the influence of their civilization engendered gradually among the Jews a relish for metaphysical speculations.

This taste was preserved, especially among the Egyptian Jews, from a necessity to extol their religion before the eyes of the Greeks.

They improved the interpretations of their Holy Scriptures, represented their articles of faith, laws and religious ceremonies, clothed with sublime aspects, in order to attain the respect of the people among whom they lived. We find already, in the Greek translation of the Pentateuch which is ascribed to " Seventy," and is known by the name Septuaginta, extending up to the times of the first Ptolemies (280–210 Before the Christian Era), numerous annotations of allegorical interpretations, and we discover therein some traces of that Greek-Oriental philosophy which developed itself since that time among the Alexandrian Jews, and whose principal representative for us is Philo.

This philosophy was already quite cultivated under the government of Ptolemy Philometor, as it can be easily ascertained by many still preserved fragments of the Jewish philosopher, Aristobul.

The Book of Wisdom, the time of the composition of which is also uncertain, but which is undoubtedly the work of an Alexandrian Jew, contains distinct traces of it.

The principal doctrine of this philosophy can be summed up as follows: The divine Being is of such an absolute perfection, that it can not be signified by any attributes which can be perceived by human thoughts.

It is an abstract Being, without any manifestation. The world is the work of certain intermediary powers, which share the divine essence, and by which alone God makes himself known, shedding innumerable beams in every direction. By this means he is omnipresent and works everywhere without being influenced by the objects which emanate from him.

We perceive in the developments of this doctrine, just as we find it in the works of Philo, an eclectical philosophy, the elements of which are borrowed from the pre-eminent systems of the Greeks, as well as of certain Oriental theories as they prevailed at that time among Hindoo philosophers, the historical derivation of which is still not sufficiently known. Although this philosophy is really fantastical and boldly declares that God is the only active principle in the world, and every motion of our soul is affected by a divine impulse, it acknowledges nevertheless the human freedom to be unrestricted, and at the risk of appearing inconsequent, it is induced by a moral and religious interest to pay homage to the Jewish principle of free will, as it has been noticed already. The Egyptian Jews understood how to give a peculiar air to this eclectical philosophy, and cultivated it with such a success that they sometimes looked on them afterward as men who were perfect, original thinkers.

This was pushed so far that they regarded Pythagoras, Plato and Aristotle as the disciples of Jews.

The fables which are detailed by different Jewish authors concerning the relations that took place between several Greek philosophers and some Jewish sages have their origin in the national pride of some rabbis, but are very old and were propagated by heathen and Christian authors. Josephus (c. Ap I. 1, c. 22) and Eusebius (Praep. Evang. I. ix. c. 3) communicate a passage as related by Clearchus, a disciple of Aristotle, that Aristotle made the acquaintance of a Jew in Asia, with whom he conversed on philosophical subjects, and confessed to have learned more from him than he did from Aristotle. According to Numenius of Apamea, Plato was nothing else than an Attic-speaking Moses.

This proves that the manner of interpreting the Bible introduced by the Egyptian Jews has gained great authority. After the Battle of Ipsus (301 Before Christ) Palestine was, with the exception of a few short intervals, under the government of the Kings of Egypt. Therefore frequent intercourse must have taken place between the Jews of both countries.

Under the later government of the Syrian Kings the relish for Greek civilization and habits became so prevalent, that the Jewish religion was exposed to the greatest dangers until finally the tyranny of Antiochus Epiphanes effected an energetic reaction, produced by the Maccabees.

We can not fail to recognize the influence of the Greek dialectics upon the schools or sects which we find in their perfect development under the Maccabean princes.

The Jews of Palestine divided themselves into two sects, namely, Pharisees and Sadducees. The first adopted the time-honored religious views, doctrines and usages and endeavored thereby to ascribe to them an ancient and divine origin, claiming that they had received them from the greatest antiquity, or at least that they received even from Moses himself the system of interpretation upon which they were founded, based upon the holy texts.

Although it can not be denied that this sect sanctioned many religious views and usages which were borrowed from the Chaldeans and Persians, their system of interpretation had, nevertheless, the advantage of giving life and motion to the dead letter, of favoring progress and development of Judaism, and of opening the door to the theological and philosophical speculations among intelligent minds.

The Sadducees, however, who refused to accept the oral tradition, and rejected all the doctrines which are not explicitly mentioned in the Bible, deprived Mosaism on account of that of all the germs of development contained in it.

They went so far as to deny the immortality of the soul and the interposition of the divine Providence in human affairs as incompatible with the principle of the freedom of will.

A society of men was organized among the Pharisees, which may be called " Practical Philosophers," who adopted the religious principles and observances of Pharisaism, but endeavored always to act according to the principles of a rigid morality, which was taught by Pharisees but not strictly performed by them.   The members of this society set the example to practice virtue.   A laborious life and the greatest frugality recommended them even to the respects of the common people, who could only judge them superficially.   They were called Essaer or Essenes, probably derived from the Syrian word *Asja* (physician); for it seems that they formed themselves upon the model of a society of Egyptian Jews who called themselves " Therapeutæ ;" or, according to the explanation of Philo, " Physicians of Souls."*   These Therapeutæ lived in solitude and devoted themselves to abstinence and contemplation.

---

* See my Guide, p. 77, Note 23, ed. Cincinnati, 1857.—TRANSLATOR.

Although the Essenes of Palestine had more regard to practice concerning religious matters, as well as social life, than the Therapeutæ, they, however, displayed like them a decided proneness to an ascetic and contemplative life. This is here especially of importance to us, because we consider them as the first preservers of a half-mystical and a half-philosophical doctrine, which developed itself among the Jews of Palestine at the time of the origin of Christianity. We know from Josephus (on the Jewish War, 1, 2, Chapter viii.) that the Essenes laid great importance on the names of angels and had special doctrines of which they made a mystery, not allowing them to be communicated to newly-initiated members of their society until after a certain time of probation. According to Philo (in the treatise entitled " Every Virtuous Person is Free "), the Essenes held in contempt the logical part of philosophy, and studied only that of the physical part, which treated on the existence of God and the origin of the world.

Therefore, they had tenets of philosophy wherein the doctrine of angels played an important part, besides certain metaphysical speculations. It is very probable that they cultivated in later times the doctrine which is known by the name Kabbalah, which was drawn from different sources and inspired the first founders of the Gnosis (sublime wisdom). The influence which the Jewish philosophers had on the New-Platonism in Egypt and Palestine, as well as on the Gnosis, placed the Jews in the rank of nations who participated in that spiritual movement which endeavored to blend the Oriental with the Occidental ideas. In this capacity they deserve a place in the history of philosophy.

But, although a certain originality must be admitted to the philosophy of the Alexandrian Jews and especially to the Kabbalah, the different elements of these two doctrines, especially their decided pantheistical tendency, are too little consonant to Judaism in order to give them the name of Jewish philosophy. There exists not a Jewish philosophy; but, nevertheless, the Jews may claim the merit of having been one of the intermediate members through whom the speculative ideas of the Orient were transferred to the Occident. Later on we will observe them appear again in the same part of mediation.

The first centuries of the Christian era show us the Jews in a situation which was not favorable to the spiritual progress. At first they were engaged in a political war, which terminated in the horrible catastrophe of Jerusalem; later, after a disastrous trial of Bar Kochba, when the teachers who escaped the vengeance of the Romans convinced themselves that Jerusalem could not be any more the center of the divine service and the symbol around which the dispersed remnants of the Jewish nation could unite themselves, they set themselves to work to devise expedients to strengthen the bonds by which the Jews of all countries were enabled to be preserved as a religious community.

The religious system of the Pharisees, to which the majority of the Jews were attached, did not suffice to preserve the Jews intact through the influence of the authority of the Holy Writ alone, therefore equal power was also ascribed to the interpretations and traditional developments that were hitherto handed down in the schools by oral instruction and of which only a few compositions are now extant, containing some parts which can not claim the honor of canonicity.

During the first quarter of the third century there appeared a vast collection of ancient religious laws, usages and observances of the Pharisaical school and even of those which had ceased to be applicable after the destruction of the Temple at Jerusalem. The different parts of this collection known by the name Mishnah (in the Novelles of Justinian, DEUTEROSIS) were during three hundred years supplied with notes in order to discuss them exhaustively in all their bearings.

They busied themselves at the same time with an extensive critical labor to establish irrevocably the text of the Holy Scriptures, according to authentical manuscripts, and went so far that they even counted all the letters which were contained in every book.

In the immense collections of the first five or six centuries of the Christian era, which we still possess in the Talmud as well as in the allegorical interpretations, there are very little traces of philosophical speculations. When we find therein reminiscences of the Kabbalah, which occur frequently, they concern only, so to speak, the exoterical part or the doctrine of the angels. The existence of the speculative part of the Kabbalah reveals itself to us in those books in mentioning the mysteries which are contained in the first chapter of Genesis, " Bereshith " (history of creation), and in the Mercabah (chariot) in the vision of Ezekiel. The Jews remained in the same spiritual state until the period when Mohammed and his successors brought about in Asia an immense revolution, and the spiritual monuments of the Mussulman world reacted powerfully upon the synagogue, and produced in its bosom struggles, the combatants of which needed quite other weapons than they were wont to wield in the Talmudical schools, and were now pressed to resolve questions of canonical rights, as well as of cases of conscience. Under the government of Abu-Djaafar-Almansur, second caliph of the Abassical dynasty, Anan ben David (2), one of the most distinguished Jewish teachers of the Babylonical academy, put himself at the head of a party which endeavored to set themselves free from rabbinical hierarchy, and to shake off the yoke of traditional laws. Anan promulgated the rights of reason and the principle of free inquiry. As he acknowledged, however, that tradition made the text of the Scriptures clearer, giving to Judaism the means to improve by degrees, he did not reject, like the old Sadducees, the principle of interpretation and every kind of tradition, but wanted to keep both in perfect unison with reason and the text of the Scriptures, and contended against the binding authority of many laws contained in the Mishnah. The members of this sect called themselves " Karaim " (adherents of the text), and are known in modern times by the name of " Karaites" or " Karaer."

We will not discuss in this connection the religious principles of Karaism, but we will only show its influence upon the philosophical speculations among the Jews.

Because, although it is true that the Karaites, having no stable principles, and having acknowledged no other authority than the individual opinions of their teachers, lost themselves in a labyrinth of contradictions and decisions the unraveling of which is much more difficult than those of the Talmudical discussions; yet it can nevertheless not be denied that Karaism, according to its principles, using the weapons of reason to refute rabbinism, they compelled the rabbis to take up the same arms in their defense.

Moreover, the Karaites were only qualified to establish a sound Biblical exegesis and a systematical and rational theology, supported by philosophy. Concerning the latter, the example of the Arabic Motekallemin had undoubtedly great influence upon the Karaitical teachers, who, according to their doctrine and schismatical situation, had much similarity (3) to the Mussulmanic sect of Motazalen, the founders of the Knowledge of Kalam.

The Karaitical theologians themselves adopted the name Motekallemin (see Kusari i., v., § 15) (4) and Maimonides (More Nebuchim i. i. c. 41) says explicitly that they borrowed their demonstrations from the Mussulmanic Motekallemin. By such demonstrations they affected to place the fundamental doctrines of Judaism upon a philosophical basis.

The dialectics of Aristotle, which came into vogue among the Arabians at that time, gave to the Mussulmanic and Jewish theologians their co-operation, although they wrote also partly their polemics against the philosophical dogmas of the Stagirite.

The main points which were defended in the books of the Karaitical Motekallemin were as follows: The first matter is not from eternity; the world was created and consequently it has a Creator; this Creator, God, has neither a beginning nor an end; he is incorporeal, and not limited within the boundaries of space; his knowledge comprehends all things, his life consists in intelligence and he himself is pure intelligence; he acts with a free will, and his will corresponds to his omniscience (see Kusari, v. 18.)

None of the works of the ancient Karaitic teachers were transmitted to us. The only evidence that we have that their works existed are the quotations from them which are occasionally found in later books.

One of the most renowned Karaitic Motekallemin is David ben Merwan al-Mokammes, or el-Mekammes of Rakka, in the Arabic language Irak, who flourished in the ninth century (5). His work is quoted by rabbinical authors, namely, by Bechaja and Jedaja Hapenini (Bedresi); but it seems that he did not know that this author was a Karaite (6).

By this it appears that he busied himself with such fundamental doctrines as were adopted equally by both sects, and that his works did not contain any polemics against the Rabbinites.

He maintains, among other things, as we are informed by Jephet ben Ali (in the tenth century), that man, as a microcosm, is the most perfect creature and takes a rank among angels (7). Whatever his theory of the angels may have been, this proves, however, that he ascribed to man pre-eminence and great power.

The Rabbinites, or the adherents of the Talmud, followed the example set by the Karaitic teachers, and tried to support their religious edifice with arguments which they drew from the philosophy of their times.

The first who opened this new path successfully and whose religious principles gained a certain authority among the Jews, was Sadias ben Joseph al Fajum, renowned as exegete, theologian and Talmudist, and at the same time a formidable antagonist of Karaism.

He was born at Fajum, in Egypt, in 892, and was appointed Principal of the Academy at Sora, near Bagdad, which was at that time the capital seat of Rabbinism. Having lost his office by the intrigues of some adversaries, he was, after a few years, reinstated, and died at Sora in the year 942. Among his numerous works, the only book which concerns us is entitled " On the Doctrines of Faith and the Different Opinions," or " On Religion and Knowledge," which was composed by him in the Arabic language about 933, and was translated into Hebrew by Juda Ibn Tabon in the twelfth century, in which language it is still extant in different editions. It was lately translated into German by Dr. Julius Fuerst, Leipsic, 1848. Besides the authority of the Holy Writ and tradition, Sadias acknowledges also that of reason, and announces not only the right but also the duty to investigate the religious faith; because it must be understood thoroughly on account of its own safety and perfection against assault from without.

Reason teaches, according to his opinion, the same truisms as revelation ; but the latter was nevertheless necessary to attain quicker to the highest truisms, which reason, when left to itself, could have only arrived at after great difficulties. The subjects of which he treats are generally those which are mentioned above by the Karaites, namely, unity of God, his attributes, the Creation, revelation of the Law, nature of the human soul, etc.

Some doctrines of faith of the second order which correspond less with reason, to-wit, resurrection of the dead, are adopted by him ; but he contents himself to prove it by the idea that reason is not positively against them ; on the contrary, all religious views which were popular at that time, and which have no foundation whatever in the Holy Writ—for instance, metempsychosis—were rejected and declared by Sadias as absurdities (E. V., Chap. iii., Berlin ed.)

Sadias denies the existence of Satan, or a contradictory angel, in his Commentary of Job, and shows that the sons of God and Satan which are mentioned in the prologue are men.

That was a bold view at the time of Sadias.

The polemics take up a great deal of space in the book of "Faith and Knowledge," and it concerns us herein that it acquaints us with the opinions which prevailed at that period in the domain of religion and philosophy. Thus we are informed that Jewish philosophers like the Motekallemin adopted the doctrine of atoms, which they considered to be everlasting.

Others, who could not resist the consequences of rationalism, denied all miracles and endeavored to explain them upon natural grounds.

Philosophy, however, takes in its true sense a second rank, according to Sadias' opinion.

It is in the service of religion, and is to him a simple tool for defense of religious doctrines of Judaism. The peripatetic philosophy had not as yet made a great advance among the Arabs; it first began spreading and establishing itself by the works of Farabi.

Sadias touched no other points of the peripatetic doctrine than the categories, and proved at large that they are not applicable to God (E. V., II. Chap. viii.)

His theory of the creation of matter is an assault upon the philosophy of antiquity generally.

Among the Jewish authors, the works of whom were transmitted to us, Sadias is the first who taught systematically the dogma of the creation out of nothing (*ex nihilo*), which was undoubtedly laid down already by Karaitical theologians. He does this indirectly by refuting all systems which are contrary to this dogma (**E. V. 1**, Chap. iv.) and maintained that the sole will of God was active at the creation. Furthermore, the doctrine of free will, based upon the evidence of the senses, reason, Holy Writ and tradition, was developed by Sadias in minute details (**E. V. 4**, Chaps. ii. and iii.). It would be useless to follow Sadias in his demonstrations, as they strike us very seldom by their novelty, and, besides, they concern more the theologian than the philosopher. Sadias' great merit consisted in having shown to his contemporaries that religion, far from fearing the light of reason, finds in it, on the contrary, a strong support. By this method he paved the way for the introduction of true philosophical studies among his co-religionists, and the brilliant epoch of the Spanish and Provenzal Jews. Shortly after the death of Sadias, the propagation of the philosophical writings of the eastern Arabians began in Spain. At the same time the Spanish Jews liberated themselves from the ecclesiastical authority of the Babylonian Academy at Sora.

A fortunate coincidence of circumstances put them in a position to establish a new school at Cordua and to find learned men to take an active part in its management (8) and to procure all literary apparatus which they were in need of, but which were in abundance among the Oriental Jews.

A learned Jewish physician, Chasdai ben Isaac ben Shaphruth, who was appointed physician at Court in Cordua by Abdal-Rahman III. and his son, Al Hakem II., exerted the great influence which he enjoyed to enrich the Spanish schools with all the works of Oriental Jews (9).

It is usually thought that the Mussulmanic philosophers in Spain were the teachers of philosophy of the Spanish Jews; but this opinion is only true concerning Maimonides and his followers in Christian Spain.

It is certain, however, that the Spanish Jews had already treated philosophy successfully, before this knowledge found among the Mussulmans a worthy representative.

Ibn Badja, or Ibn Badshe, who died very young, in the year 1138, was the first Spanish Arabian who studied profoundly Aristotle's philosophy.

But we find in the second part of the eleventh century a very remarkable philosopher in Spain, whose main work, which was afterward rendered into Latin, created great sensation among the Christian theologians of the thirteenth century.

We mean here him whom Thomas of Aquino, Albert the Great and others quoted by the name Avicebron, who is no other than he who is renowned among the Jews as a religious poet and philosopher by the name of Solomon ben Gabirol, of Malaga.

When we compare the quotations which were made by Albert and Thomas of Aquino from the book Fons Vitae (Fountain of Life), by Avicebron, with the extracts from the book Mekor

Chajim, by Solomon ben Gabirol, which is still extant in a Hebrew manuscript at the Parisian National Library, then the identity of both works being the offspring of the same author is proven by the strongest evidence (10).

Avicebron or Ibn Gabirol shows himself at once to have been initiated into the peripatetic philosophy. He distinguishes "matter and form" in all that exists, the connection of which is effected by motion, but he defines more accurately the ideas of matter and form than all Arabian peripatetics.

Matter, he says, is a simple capability to be, while it takes the form; the latter (the form) bounds the capability of being, making matter to be a certain expressed substance.

Besides God, who is a necessary and absolute Being, does not admit any substratum of possibility, every being is spiritual or material, composed of matter and form.

Avicebron first laid down this principle in an absolute sense, that matter be ascribed to the soul, as Thomas of Aquino said: "*Quidam dicunt quod anima et omnino substantia praeter deum est composita ex materia et forma. Cujus quidem positionis primus auctor invenitur Avicebron auctor libri fontis vitae*"—that is, some say that the soul and every substance besides God is composed of matter and form. This dogma was first laid down by Avicebron, author of the book "Fountain of Life," *quaestiones disputatae, quaest de anima* (Art. vi., ed. Lugd, p. 153a. See also Albertus, " De causis et proc. univ.," I. 1 tract 1, Chap. v.)

When Avicebron spiritualizes matter, on one side ascribing it to all spiritual substances, he gives on the other side, in a certain measure, a corporeity to the form, as he considers it as that by which matter is limited in always narrower boundaries from the form of substance unto its exact materiality. In the book " Fons Vitae " he expresses himself about it as follows: I will give you a rule by which you may gain a knowledge of forms and matters. You may imagine all classes of beings (in circles) one above the other, one comprising the other, one carrying the other, inclosed by two boundary lines, one above and one below.

All that is of these (beings) on the upper boundary line, surrounding all as general matter, is only a carrying matter (simple substratum); all which is on the lower boundary line, as the sensual form, is merely sensual form. Of that which is in the midst between the two boundary lines, the finer and higher becomes matter of the lower and coarser, the latter serves the first for a form.

It follows from this that the materiality of the world, which shows itself as matter carrying a form, of which it is carried itself, is a form in itself which is carried by an inside abstract matter of which we just now speak. In this way this matter becomes again the form of its following, until this returns to the first all comprising matter. The substance of this place is also communicated by Aquino, "Quaest. de Spiritualibus Creaturis," art. III. p. 1388.

The motion which combines matter with form has its origin from the will of the Creator, and not from his intellect, because only the latter could produce the infinite.

Matter receives from the will as much as was assigned of it to its susceptibility, but not according to the power of the will, because that which matter received from the light of the will is small in comparison to that which the will is able to create (Mekor Chajim I. V.)

This intermeddling of the will is a concession made to the religious demands by which Avicebron paid a faithful homage to the dogma of Creation announced by Judaism. Notwithstanding that, the independent course which he pursued in his philosophy could not please the Jewish theologians of that period. But later, when the peripatetic doctrine of the Arabians became prevalent in the Jewish schools, the doctrines of Avicebron were considered in regard to philosophy as heresies. Therefore, while the religious poems of Ibn Gabirol were very celebrated among the Jews, and were even adopted in the rituals of the synagogues, his book, entitled " Fountain of Life," was abandoned to utter oblivion.

A single Jewish author, Shem tob ben Palkeira, a distinguished philosopher of the second half of the Thirteenth Century, appreciated the philosophical work of Ibn Gabirol, which he quotes frequently, and from which he made copious extracts, translating them from the Arabic into the Hebrew language.

Ibn Gabirol could not exert any influence upon the Arabian philosophers in Spain. The Mussulmans did not read the works of the Jews.

Ibn Badja and Ibn Roshd were scarcely acquainted with the name of Ibn Gabirol, but he became renowned among the scholastics of the Thirteenth Century under the falsified name of Avicebron, by a Latin translation, "Fons Vitae," for which, according to Jourdain, we have to be thankful to the Archdeacon Gundisalvi (see " Recherches sur les traduct. d'Aristote,' 2d ed. p. 119.)

His influence upon certain scholastics is a fact acknowledged by some modern authors; but they still fail to enlighten us sufficiently on the subject.

Ibn Gabirol is by originality and boldness of thought an isolated appearance among the Spanish Jews, but, as we are informed by Maimonides, who was himself a Spaniard, his Jewish countrymen rejected generally both the system and the method of the Motekallemin, and zealously adopted the opinions of the properly so called philosophers or peripatetics, in so far as they were directly in contradiction with the fundamental doctrines of Judaism (Moreh Nebuchim 1, p. 1, ch. lxxi.) The theologians perceived the dangers by which Judaism was menaced through the encroachments of the philosophers.

Bechai, or Bachja ben Joseph, about the end of the eleventh century, was the first who endeavored to represent completely and systematically the morality of Judaism, in his book, entitled : " The Duties of the Heart " (Choboth Halbaboth).

He begins with a treatise on the unity of God, wherein he shows evidently a predilection for Sadias' method, although he reveals that he had a perfect knowledge of the difference of the peripatetic systems.

The superiority which he assigns to the practical morality above speculation, and his decided direction toward an ascetical manner of life, give him a certain resemblance to his contemporary, Gazali. (12)

A stronger reaction is manifest in the book " Cosri," or, more properly, " Cusari," composed by the renowned poet, Judah Halevi, in the year 1140.

This author made use of the historical fact, that a king of the Kosars or Chasars, together with a great portion of his people,(13) embraced Judaism in the second half of the eighth century, in order to give to his book the form of a dialogue between a Jewish savan and the king of the Chasars.

The latter, who dreamed that his motives, but not his deeds, were agreeable to God, conferred alternately with a philosopher, a Christian and a Mussulmanic theologian; but as none of these three were able to convince the king, he sent for a Jewish savan, who understood at once how to captivate the reason of the king, and returned an answer with such precision to every question that was put to him, that the king became perfectly satisfied, and finally embraced Judaism.

According to this sketch, Juda Halevi composed his book which contains the complete theory of the Rabbinical Judaism, and wherein he opened a regular campaign against philosophy.(14) He combats the error of those who think to suffice the demands of religion, when they endeavor to prove that reason, being left to itself, would gain, by its own study, the superior truism which we received by a supernatural revelation.

The revealed religion does not teach us anything that is directly against reason; but that we are able only through faith and a life consecrated to devotion and religious exercises to participate in prophetical inspiration and to be pervaded by the revealed truisms.

Reason can give us, indeed, arguments for the eternity of matter, for the creation of the world out of nothing; but that tradition, which was handed down from the most ancient times, and was propagated from one century to another, carried with it more power of conviction than any ingenious system of syllogisms and demonstrations that can be impugned very easily by other refuting arguments. The exercises which the religion prescribes have a profound sense and are symbols of sublime truisms.

This is not the place to give a full representation of the doctrines of Juda Halevi; but I will only remark that his extravagant ideas led him to the mysticism of the Kabbala. He considered the latter as part of tradition and ascribed to it great antiquity, so that he traced back the Sefer Yezirah even to the earliest times, and ascribed it to the patriarch Abraham.

The book, "Cusari," contributed, perhaps, to the revival of the study of the Kabbalah, which we find at once in a flourishing condition a century later.

Judah Halevi's endeavors were, indeed, not powerful enough to give a decisive blow to the study of philosophy, which had taken a new flight at that time through the works of Ibn Badja; but the movement of the reaction, the organ of which was the "Cusri," occasioned a great ferment. A certain uneasiness and insecurity of the most distinguished and independent minds reflect as from a mirror the Biblical commentaries of the renowned Abraham Ibn Ezra, wherein we find a strange medley of rational criticism and childish ideas borrowed from the Kabbala, sound thoughts worthy of a philosopher and astrological superstition.(15) But in order, if possible, to bring about a reconciliation between Judaism and philosophy, a mind was necessary which could control both and combine tranquillity and clearness, energy and depth, a man who was enabled, by an imposing knowledge and a piercing criticism, to illumine with the touch of knowledge the whole domain of religion, and to fix the boundaries of speculation and faith with precision.

The great man who took upon himself this task was Moses, son of Maimon, usually called Maimonides, born at Cordua, on the thirteenth of March, 1135, and died at Old Kairo, on the thirteenth of December, 1204.

Possessing a profound knowledge of the extensive religious literature of the Jews, he was at the same time very familiar with all profane sciences which were then accessible to the Arabian world.

He was the first who put in systematical order the shapeless and gigantic masses of Talmudical compilations, erected the religious edifice of Judaism upon a strong foundation and fixed the number of fundamental articles of faith, thus presenting a means to appropriate to one's self the whole of the system of religion; he effected, although not a full reconciliation, nevertheless, at last an approximation between philosophy and religion, and acknowledging the rights of both, and thereby secured for them mutual control and support.

The question as to what extent the endeavor of Maimonides was of advantage to the development of the Jewish theology, is foreign to the subject under consideration; but in reference to philosophy, his "Moreh" or "Guide of the Strays," although it did not distinctly produce results which made an epoch in the history of philosophy, contributed considerably to an always larger propagation of the study of the peripatetic philosophy among the Jews, and made the latter as mediators between the Arabians and Christian Europe, and exercised an incontestable influence upon the scholastic lore. Within the synagogue the "Moreh" or "Guide" had results which outlived the dominion of the peripatetic doctrine, and its influence is still perceptible nowadays.

By the study of the "Moreh," the greatest geniuses among the modern Jews—Spinoza, Mendelssohn, Solomon, Maimon and many others—were introduced into the sanctuary of philosophy.

The authority of this book became so significant that even the Kabbalists could not avoid it.

The Kabbalah endeavored to put itself in conformity with the peripatetic doctrine of the Arabians, and many master spirits of mysticism went so far as to find in the "Moreh" an esoteric sense, which corresponded to the doctrines of the Kabbalah.(16) The "Moreh" is the last phase of development of the philosophical studies among the Jews as a religious association.

It remains still for me to report the excellent works that were produced under the influence of the direction which the works of Maimonides gave to the studies of the Jews.

Christian Spain and Provence granted, to a great portion of Jews, who were exiled by the fanaticism of the Almohades from Southern Spain, a place of refuge.

Maimonides was also compelled to emigrate, and he went to Egypt. It is well known with what violent passion the kings of that dynasty persecuted the philosophers and destroyed their works.

Ibn Roshed (usually called Aben Rashid), who wrote his commentaries of the writings of Aristotle at the same time when Maimonides was engaged in Egypt composing his work, "Guide of the Strays," would have remained, perhaps, unknown to the Christian world, had not the Jews of Spain and Provence received his works with great admiration, to whom, also, Maimonides gives great praise, in a splendid manner, in his letters which he wrote in the last years of his life. The works of Ibn Roshed and of other Arabian philosophers, as well as the most scientific writings composed in the Arabic language, were translated into Latin according to the Arabic texts or according to very faithful Hebrew translations, either by learned Jews or under their dictation.

The interest which the Christian world took in those Hebrew translations, for which Latin translators could more easily be found than for those of the original Arabic writings, is evident from the fact that the Jewish translators were proteges of men of the highest rank in Christendom, among others, also, the Emperor Frederic II. (17)

But the more philosophy endeavored to spread, under the patronage of the name of Maimonides, the greater were the exertions made by its antagonists, who were terrified by its boldness to oppose its encroachments.

They did not respond any more quietly with arguments founded on reason as did the pious Juda Halevi.

Nobody would have been able to struggle with success against Maimonides, and then the parties were too distinctly stamped to be satisfied with a mere war of words.

The philosophers understood to win the undecided spirits, who could not comprehend the consequences of the agitation, and suffered themselves to be hurried away by the awe and confidence the name of Maimonides infused into their minds.

The antagonists of philosophy were greatly foreign to such studies and acknowledged the grossest views concerning the anthropomorphisms of the Bible.

In the Provence the "Guide of the Strays," by Maimonides, was translated into Hebrew by Samuel ben Tibbon of Lunel. The conclusion of this translation happened just at the time when Maimonides died. All translators and commentators of the Arabic philosophers were from the Provence, as, for instance, Jacob ben Abba Mari ben Antoli, (18) Moses Samuel, Samuel Ibn Tibon, and later, during the fourteenth century, Levi ben Gerson, Kalonimos ben Kalonimos, (19) Todros Todrosi, (20) Moses of Narbonne and others; and from this land the tocsin of alarm was sounded from south to north and from the occident to the orient.

They accused each other of heresy, and one party anathematized the other.

To describe the details of warfare, which was allayed many times, and then was again renewed with greater or lesser violence until the end of the thirteenth century, would exceed the object of this sketch; we, therefore, refer the reader who desires to gather a thorough information about it to the excellent essay of Dr. Geiger, in his periodical for Jewish theology (Vol. V., p. 82).

It suffices that this warfare took a turn giving advantage to philosophy, which received an advance even by the exasperation of its adversaries. In the year 1305, a synod of Rabbis, at the head of which was the renowned Solomon ben Adereth (chief of the synagogue of Barcelona), forbade, under penalty of excommunication, any person to begin the study of philosophy before he attained the age of twenty-five years; but, nevertheless, we observe that not long afterward the Arabic peripateticism was taught with a hitherto unprecedented boldness.

One of the most renowned men at that time, worthy to be mentioned under the promoters of philosophical studies, was Jedaja Penini, called Bedersi, also Bedarshi, because he was born in the city of Beziers.

On account of his work, entitled: "Bechinoth Olom" (Examination of the World), a book on morality which represents the nothingness of this world in a very sublime and racy Hebrew style, he wore the appellation, "The Eloquent."

This work gained the attention of Christian *literati* and was translated into many languages.

Jedaja shows therein that true happiness of man can only be gained by religious exactitude and knowledge, and concludes with an admonition to the reader to take for a guide the doctrines of the greatest teacher of the synagogue, namely, Moses ben Maimon—Maimonides.

In an apology, directed to Solomon ben Adereth, Jedaja defends zealously the philosophical studies against the ban under which the Rabbis of Barcelona put them.

There is still a translation, by Jedaja, of a treatise by Farabi, entitled, "De intellectu et intellecto;" and many other philosophical writings.

Joseph Ibn Caspi, of Caspe, in Aragonia, is the name of another philosopher of that time, under whose numerous works we find commentaries of Maimonides' "Guide of the Strays," and an abridged contents of the "Organon," by Aristotle. (22)

But the philosopher and exeget, Levi ben Gerson, of Bagnols (near Gerona, on the Spanish boundary), called Master Leon (among the Jews Ralbag), undoubtedly one of the greatest peripatetics during the fourteenth century, and also the boldest of all Jewish philosophers,(23) eclipsed all his contemporaries. His

works received great approbation among his co-religionists, and
nearly all were published in many editions. This success is the
more astonishing as the author explicitly acknowledged the
philosophy of Aristotle as an absolute truism, without using the
caution of Maimonides, and contorted the spirit of the Bible as
well as the tenets of faith in order to fit them to his peripatetic
ideas. It almost seems, that on account of his great merits
about the exegesis, they pardoned him for overstepping the proper
boundaries as a philosopher and theologian. And it is also
possible, that in a time when a decline of the study of philosophy prevailed and combats were discontinued, they busied
themselves with reading the ample works of Levi ben Gerson,
which attract by the easiness of style and diversity of contents
without comprehending their full scope.

He composed very extensive Biblical commentaries, wherein
a considerable portion is occupied by a philosophical interpretation. His real philosophical works are as follows:

1. Commentaries, not of Aristotle, as it reads usually in the
bibliographical rabbinical writings, but of the middle commentaries and some translations or analyses of Ibn Roshd.*

2. Milchamoth Adonaj (the wars of God) has a philosophical theological contents, wherein the author develops his
philosophical system, which is generally the pure peripateticism
as it represents itself among the Arabian philosophers, and
wherein he endeavors to prove that the doctrines of Judaism
perfectly agree with that system.

---

* These are for the most part among the manuscripts of the Parisian
National Library. All of that which relates to the Isagoge (preface) of
Porphyrius, to the categories and to the treatise, "On the interpretation,"
is translated into Latin by Jacob Mantino, and is printed in the first
volume of both Latin editions of the works of Aristotle, with the commentaries of Averroe.

He finished this work on the eighth of January, 1329, and divided it into six books, which treats of the nature and immortality of the soul, of the knowledge of the future and the prophetical spirit, of God's knowing of particular and accidental things, of the divine providence, of the celestial bodies and of the creation.

In the edition of Riva di Trento, 1560, is omitted the first division of the fifth book, which forms for itself an extensive astronomical treatise, and contains various computations and observations peculiar to the author. (24) Among those Jewish philosophers of the Middle Ages, the works of which are handed down to us, Levi ben Gerschon is the first who ventured to combat candidly the dogma of the creation out of nothing (ex nihilo).

After an extensive demonstration that the world could neither have taken its origin in an absolute nothing nor in a certain matter (Wars of God I. vi., 1 division chap. xvii.), he arrives at the conclusion that it originated in nothing and at the same time in something. This something is the first matter, which, being without any form, is withal nothing. By similar judgments and inferences he endeavored to put (25) in unison his philosophy with the handed-down dogmas concerning many other questions.

A less prolific author than Levi ben Gerson, but not a less profoundly learned peripatetic, was Moses ben Joshua, of Narbonne,(26) whose posthumous works have an essential interest for the historian of philosophy.

His commentaries of the most eminent Arabian philosophers contain a great mass of useful references and are very instructive.

He expounded the book "Makazid," by Gazali ;(27) the treatise on "the material intellect and the possibility of conjunction,"

by Ibn Roshd, in the year 1344 ;(28) the "physical treatise," of
the same author, and especially " Tractat de subtantia orbis,"
in the year 1349 ;(29) Chai Ibn Jocktan, by Tophail (in the same
year) ;(30) and the "Moreh" of Maimonides (1355 until 1362).
(31) Besides he quotes a commentary which he wrote "of the
physics " (probably of the middle commentary of Ibn Roshd).
(33)*

Moses of Narbonne has a concise and sometimes an obscure
style. His opinions are not less bold than those of Levi ben
Gerson ; but he does not express them with the same clearness
and frankness. Our attention is drawn at the same time anew
to the "Orient," by a member of the Caraitic sect, of which we
lost sight of since the tenth century.

Aaron ben Elia, of Nicomedia, residing probably in Kairo,
finished, in the year 1346, a work on philosophy of religion,
entitled : " Tree of Life," which could be ranged on the side of
the excellent "Moreh" of Maimonides, whom our author took
as a model and from whom he borrowed a great deal. Both
works breathe the same spirit, both assign to reason and philosophical speculation a considerable share in the domain of
theology.

Aaron's works give us more accurate disclosures about the
Arabian sects than the " Moreh ; " and, therefore, it is in regard
to that of great interest to him who makes historical researches.
This work was published in Hebrew by Professor Delitzsh, with
very learned prolegomena and fragments of Arabian authors,
which are highly important to the history of philosophy.

The fifteenth century shows us still some very remarkable
Jewish scholastics, but at the same time the decline of the peri-

---

* These commentaries are all extant in different manuscripts in the
National Library at Paris. There is also a treatise of our author (" On
the soul and its abilities ").(32)

patetic philosophy and a return to doctrines which correspond more with the spirit of Judaism.

In the year 1425, Joseph Albo became renowned by his work, entitled : " Iccarim " (book of fundamental doctrines of Judaism). He reduced therein the thirteen articles of faith, laid down by Maimonides, to three fundamental doctrines; the existence of God, revelation and immortality of the soul. (34) The dogma of immortality must be considered as the substance of the third cardinal doctrine, to which Albo gives more extension ; because he comprises in the words reward and punishment, retribution generally in this world as in the next. This work makes an epoch in Jewish theology; but is merely, for the history of philosophy, of subordinate advantage.

Abraham Bibago, at Hueska, in Aragonia, composed, in 1446, a commentary of the "Last Analysis" (Aralytica posteriora of Aristotle).(35)

He resided later, about 1470, at Saragossa,(36) and became renowned as a theologian by a work, entitled : " The Path of Faith."

Joseph ben Shem Tob, whose father wrote against philosophy and even against Maimonides, became known by different theological and philosophical works, among which must be (37) mentioned an ample commentary of " Ethics to Nikomachus," which he composed at Segovia, 1455, and another of the treatise, " On the material reason," by Ibn Roshd.

His son, Shem Tob, wrote philosophical essays " On the first matter," " On the final cause," and commentaries of Maimonides " Moreh," and of the " Physics " of Aristotle,(38) 1480.

At the same time there lived, in Italy, a renowned Jewish philosopher by the name of Elias del Medigo, who was teacher of philosophy in Padua, and Pic de la Mirandola was one of his disciples.

He composed for the latter some philosophical writings, namely, an essay "On intellect and prophecy," (1482), and a commentary of the treatise, "De substantia orbis," by Ibn Roshd (1485). His questions about several philosophical subjects were published in the Latin language.

In a little Hebrew work, entitled, "Examination of the Law" (that is of the religious law), which he composed in 1491, he tried to prove that the study of philosophy can not injure the religious feelings; but one must know very well to discriminate between that which belongs to the domain of philosophy and that which belongs to religion.(39)

The expulsion of the Jews from the whole Spanish monarchy, which happened at the close of the fifteenth century, destroyed the center of the Jewish civilization at that time. On the other side, the decline of the scholastic lore effected the annihilation of the philosophical studies among the Jews, as the latter languishing everywhere from severe oppression, they could not participate in the new spiritual life which was spreading in Europe.

The civilization of the Spanish Jews died out without having been replaced soon by a new one.

We hear still some echo of Jewish scholastic lore; here and there noticeable eminent men among the Spanish emigrants, as, for instance, the renowned Isaac Abarvanel and his son Juda; but the history of Jewish philosophy (if such an expression may be used) is now really closed.

The Jews, endeavoring to bring the Arabian philosophy in conformity with their religion, gave the peripatetic doctrine an especial character, by which it became for them, in some respects, a national philosophy.

If there have been since then some philosophers among the Jews, they belong to the history of a universal civilization, and are not to be regarded as philosophers of their particular creed. Spinoza, who philosophized without any regard for the religious feelings of a congregation consisting mostly of Spanish and Portuguese refugees, sacrifices of the inquisition, which felt no sympathy for men who suffered so much on account of their belief, was disowned by the Jews.

Even Moses Mendelssohn, who interested himself so nobly for the cause of his co-religionists, and on whom we look as the creator of the modern civilization of the European Jews, he would and could not establish for them a new philosophical era. In fine, the Jews as a nation, or as a religious association, play only a secondary part in the history of philosophy, because this was not their mission.

They, however, in conjunction with the Arabs, indisputably partake of the merit of having preserved and promulgated the philosophical knowledge during the centuries of barbarism, and have exercised for a long time a civilizing influence on the European world.

NOTES OF THE AUTHOR.

No. 1. Even Arabic authors adopted the erroneous opinion, that Greek philosophy was borrowed from the Jews. See "Treatise on Animals," by Kalonimos ben Kalonimos, which contains an extract from an Arabic Encyclopœdia, entitled: " Resail ikhwan alcafa," or " Treatise of the Brothers of Purity," translated into Hebrew. Again, Ichwan-os-suffa, in the original Arabic, Calcuth, 1812; page 214.

No. 2. Anan, founder of Karaism, flourished certainly under the Califate of Abu Djafar al Mansur, in the year 136 of the Hegira, 754 of the Christian era. See the book (מטה אלהים) a Hebrew manuscript of the Parisian National Library, No. 61.

No. 3. In regard to the doctrines of the Arabian scholastics, comprising the Motazales (מעתזלה) as well as the Asharites (אשעריה), must be remarked that the latter were absolute fatalists, while the Motazales, who conceded that man had a free will and acknowledged the justice of God, maintain that man does good or evil of his own accord. They also agreed not to admit any attributes separated from the divine being, and avoided by that all which could be prejudicial to the dogma of the unity of God. On account of these two principal points of their doctrine, they assumed the name " Retainers of Justice and Unity," and exactly the same expressions are used by Masudi, an Arabian historian of the tenth century, in order to signify the disciples of Anan. See " Notices et extraits des manusc. T. viii., p. 167, 168. Silv. de Sacy, "Chrest Arabe," T. I. p. 349–51.

The Karaite, Aaron ben Elias, says, explicitly. that the Karaitic, as well as a part of the Rabbinical philosophers, are followers of the principles of the Motazales. (See עץ חיים A. b. El. System der religioesen Philosophie v. F. Delitzsch, Leipzig, 1841 ; 8 p. 4.)

No. 4.   When the King of the Chasars asked the savant to represent to him the substance of the dogmas of the Caraitic philosophers, he expressed himself about it, according to the Arabic original (manuscript in the Bodleian Library), as follows : " I desire to know some summary fundamental principles of the views of the Okulijim, or of those who judge of the fundamental principles, called, by the Karaites, masters of the knowledge of Kalam (speech or word).

No. 5.   In the book, entitled : " Eshkol Hakofer," by the Karaite Juda Hadassi, is mentioned our David Al-Rakki.   He was called so because he was undoubtedly born in the city of Rakka or Racca.

No. 6.   Bechai, or Bachje, when enumerating the different classes of religious writings, expressed himself in the preface of his book, "On the duties of the heart," as follows : " The third class causes to strengthen the religious subjects in the minds by arguments and refutation of heretics, as the book ' On faith and knowledge,' by Sadias ; the book ' On the fundamental principles of the Law,' and the book 'Almokames,' and such like." " In the same sense," says Jedaja Penini, in his apologetic writing, כתב התנצלות concerning the Moreh Nebuchim directed to Rabbi Solomon ben Adereth, " Rabbi David Hababli, called Al Mokames, from whom we have a book which was entitled after his surname, wherein he endeavors, by a careful inquiry, to give arguments for well-known principles of faith, and to combat by that the opinions and refutations of heretics."

The book, "Al-Mokammes," which was composed in the Arabic language, contained twenty chapters ; three of them were traced out in the Hebrew language not long ago, and were published by Professor Fuerst. The second contained the ninth and the third a part of the tenth chapter. The same fragments, with the exception of the latter, were published by A. D. Luzatto, in Halichoth Kedem, by Pollak. Amsterdam, 1847.

[Dr. B. Beer, in his German translation of this book, remarks that Professor Steinschneider communicated to him that Moses ben Esra quoted also the twenty chapters of "Al-Mokammes Alrakki.—Translator.]

No. 7. From two places of Jephet's commentaries on Gen. i. 26 and Psalm viii. 6, it seems evident that David ben Merwan belonged to the Karaitic sect, which is doubted by Professor Fuerst and others. Jephet, who lived in the tenth century, must have known the truth. The criticism which he makes there, concerning David ben Merwan, would have been severer had he directed it against a Rabbinist, and he would not have failed to cry at his heresy.

No. 8. Compare Abraham ben David, in "Sefer Hakabalah," ed. Amsterdam, p. 41 *b*., about some *literati* who were taken prisoners on the Mediterranean Sea, by the captain of a ship of Abd-al Rahman III., two of whom were ransomed by the Jewish congregation at Cordova.

No. 9. Abn Jussuf Chasdai ben Isaac, whose family name was Shafrut or Shaprut, was one of those fortunate men who know how to gain, by genius and knowledge, a high station in life, by which they become powerful protectors of their oppressed brethren; because it is a gross mistake when one believes that the Jews residing in Mussulmanic Spain generally enjoyed equal rights with the dominant tribe or were safe from persecution and debasement. Chasdai had a great credit with Abd-al-Rahman III. His expressions concerning it, in a letter directed to Joseph, King of the Chasars, in the year 950, are published in the preface of the book "Kusari," in some editions, and are confirmed by some Arabian authors.

The physician, Ibn Djoldjol, at Cordova, who lived under the government of Hesham II. (976–1001), mentioned our Chasdai among the physicians of Abd-al-Rahman, and speaks of the particular credit he had with this King, and that he used zealously his high position to serve the sciences by co-operating to complete an Arabian translation of Dioscorides. See Silv. de Saci "Relation de l'Egypte par Abdallatif," p. 497 et 500. Ibn Abi Oceibia, who preserved for us the above quotation of Djoldjol, in his "History of the Physicians," and took particular notice of "Chasdai," which was not yet printed, we will give here a translation of it. "Chasdai ben Isaac, well posted in the science of medicine, was in the service of Al-Hakem, son of Abd-al-Rahman, who was called Al-Nacir Ledin-allah. Chasdai ben Isaac belonged to the Jewish literati, who held the first rank concerning the knowledge of their law; he opened, for his co-religionists in Andalusia, the gates of knowledge of the religious jurisprudence, chronology, etc.

Previous to that time, they had to address themselves to the Jews in Bagdad concerning suits, calendars and the time of festivals; they had to send to them for the computation of a certain number of years in behalf of the calendar procedure and the New Year's days. But when Chasdai was appointed by Al-Hakem, who gave him a high situation, he succeeded in procuring for himself, from the Jews in the Orient, all the books which he wanted. Since that time the Jews in Andalusia knew that which before was unknown to them, and were spared all the trouble they had previously to undergo.

A Christian author at that time mentions also our Chasdai, on the occasion of an embassy, which the German Emperor Otto I. sent to Cordova, 953. Abd-al-Rahman III. wanted to know the main object of the mission before he would receive the embassadors, and commissioned Chasdai to hold a private interview with Abbot John von Goerz. (See "Vita Jonnis abbat. Gorziensis," by Labbe, nova bibliotheca manusc. lib. T. I., p. 772. Holland, "Acta Sanctor.," T. III., p. 713. "Pertz monumenta Germaniæ historica," T. IV., p. 371 and 372.)

No. 10. I entered already into particulars in Lit. Bl. d. Or., 1846, No. 46, to prove that Avicebron, who was mentioned by Ritter among the Arabian philosophers, was no other than the Jewish poet, Ibn Gabirol. The renowned historian of philosophy acknowledged the correctness of my arguments, and expressed this explicitly in an essay contained in the "Goettinger gelehrten Anzeigen," April 17, 1847. At the close of that article Professor Ritter says: "I certainly believed that the philosophy of the Middle Ages owed no thanks to the Jewish philosophers for a fertile influence, but Mr. Munk's discovery reclaimed me from this error."

No. 11. Shemtob ben Joseph ben Palquera, or Falquera, a Spaniard, was born between 1224 and 1228. In the preface of one of his works (Mebakesh), composed in October, 1263, he says he has already passed half of seventy years and is about forty years of age. All his works evince his extensive and profound learning, and especially his thorough knowledge of the philosophical works of the Arabians. His commentaries of the whole Bible, which he himself quoted (see preface of "Moreh hamoreh"), were not transmitted to us, but the following books were, of which he composed the five first ones before he was thirty-five years of age. They are:

1st. אגרת בתי הנהגת הגוף והנפש Treatise written in verses on the conduct of the body and soul. Manusc. in the Medizäic Library at Florence.

2d. צרי הינון "Balm of sorrow," or "On the resignation and

power of the soul in misfortune." Published at Cremone, 1550, at Prague, 1612.

[Dr. B. Beer remarks that the main contents of this book, which was published in Cremona, was not composed by Shem-tob, but that the greater part of the text, as well as the comments thereon, were those of a certain person called Saul, who was in possession of an original copy, and having lost it, composed the book entirely from memory. The main contents of the book correspond with that of Palquera.—Translator.]

3d. אגרת הויכוח Colloquy of a theologian and philosopher concerning the reconciliation of religion with philosophy. Published at Prague, 1610, 8.

4th. ראשית חכמה "The beginning of wisdom," or "Guide in sciences." This work consists of three sections: the first treats of moral qualities which ought to be possessed in order to begin the study of sciences and philosophy; the second contains a review of all sciences; and the third discusses the necessity of philosophical studies in order to gain true happiness. A manuscript of this work is in the Vatican, and in the Parisian National Library there is a Latin translation of it, and before that is also a translation of the work No. 3, Manusc. No. 6691 a.

5th. ספר המעלות " The book on the ranks," or "Treatise on the degrees of human perfection and on the more or less perfect societies." Manusc. in the Paris National Library, suppl. heb. No. 15, wherein is also contained the above-mentioned work No. 3.

6th. המבקש "The Searcher" (after knowledge). Review of human knowledge. Composed 1263, in an elegant style, rhymed prose intermingled with verses. Published, Amsterdam, 1779, 8.

7th. ס' הנפש Book on the soul in twenty chapters, according

to the principles of the Arabian peripatetics. Manusc. No. 239 Hebrew manusc. of the Parisian National Library.

8th. שלמות המעשים Perfection of works. A small moral treatise of ten chapters (It is in the same manuscript with No. 7.)

9th. מורה המורה Commentary on the philosophical places in Maimonides' "Moreh;" composed in 1280. It is of great utility for the study of the Arabian philosophy. In the appendix are amended many places of Ibn Tibbon's translation according to the Arabian original, published at Presburg (by Bissliches) 1837–8. Manusc. in the Paris National Library.

10th. "Apologetic writing for the Moreh," by Maimonides, who was assailed anew by some French Rabbis in 1290. It is printed at the close of the work מנחת קנאות Presburg, 1833–8. Manusc. at the close of the above-mentioned work—No. 9.

11th. Extracts from the work מקור חיים "Source of life," by Solomon Gabirol, which he translated from the Arabic language into Hebrew. Heb. Manusc., of the Parisian National Library, No. 239. The author mentions in his preface of the "Meba-kesh," besides all these works, two books more which he has composed: אגרת המוסר "Writing on morality," and מגלת הזכרון "Scroll on memory," or "Recollections," of which we find no trace anywhere.

No. 12. Bechaja, or Bachja, who is usually supposed to have lived in the twelfth century, but who lived at the end of the eleventh century, as it is proved by Rappaport in his biography of Rabbi Nathan, p. 42, note 40; because as our author, when quoting all the different compendiums of the Talmud, did not make any mention of that by the distinguished Rabbi, Isaac Alfasi, who died 1103. The name Bechai must be pronounced Bachja or Bachje, as Menasse ben Israel and other Jewish Spanish authors pronounce it; as, for instance, the author of the poetical translation of the "Chobot halbaboth," published in Amsterdam, 1670.

No. 13. According to the report of Masudi, this conversion took place at the time of the Kalif Harun-al-Rashid. See El-Masudi's historical encyclopædia, entitled, "Meadows of Gold," etc., translated from the Arabic by A. Sprenger, v. I., p. 407. It is to be regretted that we no longer possess the works from which Masudi has drawn the communications about the particulars of the conversion of the King of the Chasars.

At a period when stupid hatred and unreasonable prejudices played the part of criticism, where the Jews were concerned Christian authors, as Buxtorf, Basnage, Baratier, etc., scoffed at the Jews on account of their statement that the Jewish religion occupied a throne during many centuries in the Middle Ages. Basnage even says: "One may search for the empire of the Chasars very far and he will find it nowhere (Hist. d. J. I. VII., chap. 1, § 14.) It required the evidence of Arabian authors to prove the great exactness of the Jewish communications, and especially of the answer and all its particulars, which was sent by Joseph, King of the Chasars, to Chasdai ben Joseph.

A full description of the Chasars in the tenth century, according to Arabian authors, is to be found in the excellent works by d'Ohsson, "Des peuples du Caucase, au Voy d'Abou El-Casem." Paris, 1828, 8, chaps. 2 and 3.

[Dr. B. Beer remarks : "Compare, also, concerning the Chasars, 'History of Russia,' by Karamsin ; German by Trappe, Dresden, Arnold, vol. I., p. 11. See also 'Maggarische Alterthuemer,' by S. Cassel, Berlin, 1848."—Translator.]

No. 14. Juda Halevi expressed himself energetically in his poems against the Greek philosophy, which he claims to proffer many blossoms but no fruits. "Having heard," says he, "the abstruse words of philosophy constructed upon a weak foundation, one returns with an empty heart and the mouth filled with phrases and idle talk." (See " Bethulath bath. Jehudah," by Luzatto, Prague, 1840, p. 56.)

No. 15. Ibn Ezra, renowned among the Jews as one of the most rational and boldest commentators of the Bible, was in the Middle Ages not less distinguished on account of his astrological knowledge, so that he was considered as one of the most learned of this chimerical knowledge, for which he wrote a series of works that were formerly much appreciated. Petrus Paduanus translated them into Latin, in the year 1293. (Maunsc. of the Paris National Library No. 7348.) The Hebrew originals are also in manuscript in the same library.

The books, העולם 'ס and הטעם 'ס המולרות 'ס were published under different editorships, which were known to Pico de la Mirandola. Compare his "Disput. in Astrologiam I.," viii., c. 5. He quoted the first edition of the book, "Astrologicis rationibus" (הטעמים 'ס) and adds : "Conscripsit enim (Avenezra) de eadem re libros duos."

No. 16. Compare Maimonides' letter to his disciple Joseph Not. sur Jos. ben Jehuda, "Journal asiat.," Juil, 1842, p. 31.

No. 17. Jacob ben Abba-Mari, residing at Neapel, says, in a transcript of his translation of the middle commentary of Ibn Roshd on the "Organon," which he finished 1232, that he was receiving a pension from the Emperor, who, as he adds, "loves the sciences and all who occupy themselves with them."

No. 18. Or better, "Anatolio" אנטולי as it reads sometimes in manuscripts, namely, in No. 207 de l'ancien fonds, in the continuation of the translation of the extract of the "Almagest," by Ibn Roshd.

No. 19. Kalonymos was born in 1287, as it appears by many remarks at the close of many works which he translated. Concerning this author, compare Zunz in "Geiger's Zeitschrift," vol. II., p. 313–320; vol. IV., p. 199–201. He has certainly composed also Latin translations, as the author of " Sifthe Jeshenim" cites. This name is identical with Calo Kalonymos, who translated into Latin the " Destructio destructionis," and many other treatises by Averrois. At the beginning of a manuscript of אבן בוחן (fonds des Oratorium No. 24) he is explicitly called מאישטרו קאלו (Master Kalo).

No. 20. Todros is a translator of a commentary, by Ibn Roshd, on "Rhetoric and Poetry of Aristotle," which work is dated Trinquetaille, near Arles, 1337.

No. 21. We can not pass over in silence two more meritorious men—Jacob ben Machir, of Montpellier, and Samuel ben Jehuda, of Marseilles. The first lived at Montpellier in the second half of the thirteenth century and the first years of the fourteenth century. He composed translations of a great many philosophical and mathematical works from the Arabic, as well as having written many very esteemed astronomical treatises which were translated into Latin. He was also called Profiat or Profatius, and under this name he was also known among Christians.

Wolf (Bibl. Hebr. vol. I., p. 988; vol. III., p. 914) has erroneously presented Profatius and Jacob ben Machir as two different authors. The treatise quoted by Wolf de Quadrante, in the Parisian National Library, Latin Manusc. No. 7437, is merely a literal translation of the Hebrew treatise, רובע ישראל by Jacob ben Machir.

Samuel ben Jehudah ben Meshullam was born 1294, and was usually known (according to his own statements) by the name, of Miles of Marseilles. His grandfather, Meshullam was a great grandchild of Jacob ben David Profiague, who is mentioned, by Benjamin of Tudela, as one of the richest residents of Marseilles, and who, according to the appendix of "Shebet Jehudah," died in 1170. Samuel devoted himself, from his eighteenth year, to the study of sciences and philosophy, studied astronomy at Salon (שלו) under the direction of Abba-Mari, usually called Sennor Astruc of Noves. In 1322 he was taken in custody with other Jews at Beaucaire. We find him, by turns, at Murcia, in Spain, at Tarascona (1329–30), Aix (1335–36), Monteil Aimart or Montelimart, 1340. The Parisian National Library possesses his translation of the treatise, "De Anima," by Alexander of Aphrodisia, of the "Almagest," by Ibn Aflah, and of an extract of the "Organon," by Ibn Roshd. At the close of the works mentioned are a few biographical particulars about Samuel ben Jehudah.

No. 22. Compare "Zunz additam. ad Catol. Lips," p. 323. From some investigations which I have made in the manuscripts in the Parisian National Library, to which Mr. Carmoli called my attention, it follows that J. Caspi, of l'Argentiere, in Languedoc, now dep. de l'Ardeche, was born there. Caspi is undoubtedly the Hebrew translation of l'Argentiere, as it was customary at that time. For instance, Lunel-Jarchi, Montpellier Hargaash. Concerning the life of Caspi, compare De Rossi Catal. cod. 755. Delitzsch and Zunz at other places. In the manuscript fond de l'orat No. 105, the author is called אבונפוש דלאנגליטרא that is, Bonafoux de l'Argentiere.

No. 23. Neither the year of his birth nor of his death is exactly known. De Rossi maintains that he was born 1288, as he found it in a manuscript of an arithmetic by Levi ben Gerson, which harmonizes well with the time of his composition of his other different works. But a remark which is at the close of a manuscript of Rashi's Bible commentary (fonds de Sorbonne No. 50) gives rise to some doubts about it. The copyist, David ben Gerson, says that he wrote this commentary for the use of his brother, Rabbi Levi, 5058 (A. M.) 1298. Now, were it proved that he meant by this Rabbi Levy ben Gerson, we must presume that he was born at an earlier period than that given by De Rossi. This manuscript, however, which is written in German characters, and therefore being improbable that it should have been written in Provence, could have been composed by one bearing the same name.

According to Juchsin, Levi ben Gerson died in 1370; but it is not probable that he lived so long, because his last works are dated 1338, and his astronomical observations do not reach beyond 1340.

We know, nevertheless, according to a few statements at the close of his works, that his literary activity began 1321 and closed 1338. although some sections of his " Milchamoth Adonaj" were already composed or sketched 1316 or 17. (Compare the edition of this work, p. 68 b.) He began with an Arithmetical work, ספר המספר which he finished April, 1321. He devoted the other part of that year and the two succeeding years to the explanation of different commentaries, by Ibn Roshd, on Aristotle. He proceeded then to elucidations of such parts of the Bible, where he could give his philosophical exegesis full scope, as Canticles, Job. the first chapter of Genesis, and Ecclesiastes. At the same time he composed also his work, " Milchamoth Adonaj." After the conclusion of that he gradually wrote commentaries on the books, " Esther and Ruth." " The Pentateuch," " The First Prophets," " Daniel," " Ezra," " Nehemiah," " The Chronicles," and at last, " The Proverbs of Solomon," which he concluded on the third (Ijar) April 23, 1338. We have reason to presume that Levi ben Gerson had his main residence in the earldom Venaissin. According to a Latin note, which we will cite afterward, he resided in the city of Orange. He went from there very often to a city, which he called Hyssop

City (עיר האזוב), in order to make astronomical observations. Many Jewish authors were called after this city, האזובי (Haesobi.)

This proves that האזוב is not the corrupted name of a city, but the Hebrew word for "hysop," which Joseph ben Caspi, author of the "Kaaroth Kesseph," signified by the words: " My name is Hyssop, but my words are Cedars." We believe that Hyssop City is identical with Avignon, although we can not understand clearly the etymological connection between Avignon and Hyssop. At the close of his commentary on "Deuteronomy," Levi ben Gerson says that he has finished this work in Hyssop City; and it is added, in a manuscript in the Parisian National Library (Anc. fonds No. 79): " When one is reading this book, he shall consider that I have composed this whole commentary in great haste in the city Avignon, without having had at hand any Talmudical or Biblical books. From this it evidently follows that " Ir haesob " was Avignon, and that Levi ben Gerson lived there at certain times. In his astronomical works we often find mentioned "Ir haesob," but once only Avignon. Probably Avignon, which was at that time the capital of the Pope, attracted our Levi ben Gerson on account of its scientific sources. [Hyssop is a plant which was used by the Jewish priest in ancient times to cleanse the lepers. Avignon being the capital of the pope, who was considered by Christians to have the power to forgive sins and to cleanse the unclean, it seems probable that the Jewish *literati* therefore called it " Hyssop."—Translator.]

No. 24. The Parisian National Library possesses three manuscripts of this work, one of which is not complete. The work consists of 136 chapters. Having prefaced by some general meditations on the advantage and difficulty of astronomy, the author portrays an instrument invented by him to make with it some astronomical observations, which he calls "The dis-

coverer of subjects that are found with great difficulty" (מגלה
עמוקות). In the ninth chapter he celebrates it in two verses. In
the continuation of the work, he shows the insufficiency of the
Ptolomeic and that of an invented system of an Arabian astron-
omer of the twelfth century. The latter is designated by the
author "Baal Techunah Chadashah," who is no other than
Abu Isak al Batrudji (Al petragius). The latter system made a
great sensation, as it appears from the book "Jesod Olam," by
Jizchak Israeli, 11, 9, where Albatrudji is called האיש המרעיש
(The Thunderer). Levi ben Gerson proves first the impossibility
of this system and gives then his own opinions about the world,
which he based on the observations he made at different times.
He concluded this work on the twenty-first of Kislew, 5089, A.
M. (November 24, 1328). He revised and improved it afterward
in different places, and added then gradually the newer observations which he made until the year 1340. This work, which
ought to occupy a place in the history of astronomy, deserves
to be examined by a professional man.

Pico de la Mirandola quoted it many times in his "Disputa-
tiones in Astrologiam," and expresses himself about it as follows (1, ix., c. 8): "Leo Hebraeus, a distinguished man and
renowned mathematician, who doubted the ancients, invented a
new instrument, the excellent construction of which we can see
by its mathematical accuracy."

Wolf (Bibliotheca Hebr. 1, p. 436) took this Leo Hebraeus
for the son of Isaak Abravanel. The part (c. 4, 11) which
treats of the instrument mentioned formed formerly a separate
work and was translated into Latin for the Pope Clemens VI.,
1342, which translation (Parisian National Library Manusc. lat.
No. 7293) concludes with the remark: "Explicit tractatus in-
strumenti astronomiae magistri Leonis Judaei de Balneolis
habitatoris Auraycae (which is Orange). Ad summam Ponti-

ficem Dominum Clementem VI. translatus de Hebraeo in La-
tinum anno incarnationis Chr. et. pontificatus dicti domini
Clementis anno primo."

No. 25. The bold views of Levi ben Gerson, as well as his
peripatetic interpretations of holy Scriptural passages and
religious dogmas were a subject of the greatest criticism by the
orthodox Rabbis.

Isaac Abravanel bewails, in several writings, and especially
in the commentary on Joshua (chap. 10), the errors of Jewish
philosophers, who presume that there is a primitive matter, that
they put the active intellect on God's place, deny the divine
providence concerning the individual man, and maintain that the
immortality of the soul is only a reunion with the active intellect (שכל הפועל). He complains especially of Levi ben Gerson,
who, as he says, did not consider it necessary even to veil his
thoughts, but announced them with the greatest clearness, and
expressed his ideas about the first matter, חומר הראשון the soul,
the prophecy and wonders in such a way and manner that it
would be a sin merely to hear it, much more to believe in it.
Before Abravanel, Isaac ben Shesheth spoke of Levi ben Gerson
in the same strain (1374), but with more respect.

No. 26. Moses ben Joshua, with the surname " Master Vidal,"
was a descendant of a family which came from Narbonne, but
resided in Perpignan, in which latter city young Moses applied
himself to his studies under the direction of his father (compare his commentary on the " Moreh" I., 1 c. 50 and 63). We
can not state exactly the time of his birth, but we may presume
that it was probably in the last year of the thirteenth or the first
years of the fourteenth century. About the date of his death
there is a doubtful intimation in a manuscript of the Parisian
National Library (fonds de l'Oratoire No. 40), whose last pages
contain a small treatise, "On the free will," composed by our

Moses to refute a writing entitled אגרת הגזרה wherein a contem-
poraneous man of letters, whom our Moses did not mention by
his name, defended fatalism. The treatise was concluded by
Moses at Sorla, Friday, on the twelfth of Tebeth, 5122, A. M.,
December 10, 1361, and has the following heading: המאמר
כבחירה לר משה הנרבוני וחברו כמשלש חדשים טרם פטירתו. "The treatise
on the free will was composed by Rabbi Moses of Narbonne
about three months before his death." By this it appears that
the author died in the year 1362, that the words, "about three
months," are not to be taken literally, because we know that
Moses concluded his commentary on the "Moreh" on the 1st
of Ijar, April 26, 1362. In the latter work (I. iii., chap. 17) he
cites his small treatise on fatalism, on account of which some
doubts arise about the authenticity of the above date.

Be it as it may, there is no work by Moses of Narbonne later
than 1362. But he must have been at that time in a very ad-
vanced age, because he relates, in a postscript (see his commentary on the "Moreh"), that his son Joshua urged him to con-
clude this work that they may not after his death reproach him
for having neglected the greatest philosopher of his own nation,
while, on the other hand, he had written commentaries on the
works of foreign philosophers. See, concerning Moses of Narbonne, Zunz addit. ad catal. cod. Lips. to which these notices
may serve as a supplement. His commentary on the "Lamentations" of Jeremiah (addit. p. 326) was one of his former
works. It is in the Parisian National Library (anc. f. 280). He
speaks therein of his design to write a commentary on אפשרת
הדבקות "On the possibility of the Union with the Eternal" (by
Averroes).

No. 27. This work is entitled, in the Hebrew, כונות הפלוסופים
"Intentio philosophorum," and was one of his first literary
works. (Compare Zunz add. p. 326, col. 8, et Delitzsch cat. p.

305.) According to Casiri (Bibl. Arab. hisp. T. I., p. 184), it seems that there is in Escurial an Arabic commentary by our author on "Tehafot," by Gazali, but it appears to me not probable, and rests upon an error.

No. 28. Compare Delitzschii cat. cod. Heb. Lips. p. 308, and Zunz addit. p. 325. According to the report in all manuscripts, Moses concluded his work, "Thamus," the 7th, 4104 (June 19, 1344). This was, however, on a Saturday. This must, therefore, be undoubtedly a mistake.

This commentary was composed in the midst of the war troubles which took place (in the region of Roussillon) between Peter IV., King of Aragonia, and his brother-in-law, Jacob, King of Majorka, as the author himself expresses it explicitly. (See Delitzsch I. c.)

No. 29. The physical dissertations, entitled, (הדרושים הטבעיים) form a collection of small treatises and simple remarks of Ibn Roshd, on many different questions which he annexed to the physics of Aristotle. One part of them, with a commentary of Moses Narbonne, is in the Parisian National Library, manusc. 8, No. 118 fonds de l'Orat. Another part of them, under the title, מאמר בעצם הגלגל "De substantia orbis," is contained in No. 96, 122, 2° of the same fonds.

The commentary of the latter collection, which concludes the dissertations, was finished on the 5th of Adar, 5109 (Feb. 24, 1349). In the preface of the commentary on the first collection (No. 118) the author says, who retired to Cervera, in Catalonia, that he had undertaken this work at the requests of his friends, the *literati* of Perpignon, in order to preserve his literary connection with them.

He called, later, these learned men כת האחים (Society of brethren), and in the preface of Chai Ibn Jocton (see the following remark), he called them נכבדי החבורה מדורשי החכמה אשר בעיר פרפניאן

" Esteemed inquirers for knowledge in the City of Perpignon," causes us to presume that here is spoken of a literary society which was within the Jewish congregation in the City of Perpignon. He mentions also the great tribulations which befell many congregations at that time, the devastation of the Jewish congregation of Cervera, by which he himself lost the greater part of his library.

No. 30. That the date of the Leipzig manuscript is false was already proved by Zunz, 1 c. The most manuscripts, among which are two of the Parisian National Library, give the date of the conclusion of this work of Cervera the evening before Pentecost, the fourth of Sivan, for the 5th was on Saturday, 5109 (May 22, 1349). This commentary facilitates the comprehending of the text by Ibn Tofail, and gives valuable explanations of the doctrines of Arabian philosophers.

At the close, the commentator gives an analysis of an interesting work by Abu Bekr al Cajeg, or Ibn Badja, entitled : בהנהגת המתבודד (" The manner of a recluse ") which work he discovered when, on account of the war, he had to flee to Valenzia· Since the original work is no longer extant, the analysis is therefore the more valuable. The statement of Zunz (1 c. p. 326, No. 6) must be amended according to this.

No. 31. The author says, in a postscript, that he commenced this commentary at Toledo and concluded it, after seven years, in Soria. Several circumstances, among which was especially the plundering which he suffered on the second day of Pentecost, 5115, A. M. (May 18, 1355), forced him to discontinue his work.

It appears from a passage, 1, ii. c. 47, of a commentary, that he sojourned since 5118 (1358) at Soria, where as he relates he saw a Christian woman who was one hundred and thirty years of age. At the close of that postscript is given the date of the conclusion of his commentary, the 3d Ijar, 5122 (April 26, 1362), when he intended to return to his native country.

No. 32. (Compare Zunz 1 c. p. 325, col. 2, No. 2). This treatise, entitled: "שלמות הנפש" ("Perfection of the Soul") is in manuscript in the Parisian National Library (fonds de l'orat. No. 118). The author composed this treatise for his son, in order to replace to him, on this subject, the works of Aristotle and Ibn Roshd. As a preface, he repeats the first book of Aristotle's "Treatise on the soul," according to its treatment in the middle commentary of Ibn Roshd.

Moses' own treatise begins with the second part and is divided into five books: on the soul and its abilities, the material or passive intellect, the opinions of the commentators about it, especially the ideas of Ibn Roshd, and, finally, on the active intellect (שכל הפועל) and on God. the first cause of all motion (סבה הראשונה).

The author confesses that there are therein many repetitions taken from his treatise "On the material intellect." (See above.)

It is therefore proved that he composed later the treatise "On the soul." A reference which is made in the treatise, "On the material intellect," to his book, "On the soul," must therefore be a later addition of the author.

The book, "On the soul," is older than the "Commentary on physical dissertations," and was consequently composed between 1344 and 1349.

No. 33. In the beginning of the preface of his dissertations, he cites this commentary with the words: פירוטנו כפרישת שמע טבעי לבן רשד

In the postscript (see commentary) on the "Moreh," he cites also his works or commentaries on logic and metaphysics, and in the commentary itself (I. i. c. 55), see פרקי משה (Capita Mosis), probably a collection of philosophical aphorisms.

No. 34. Compare, however, the elaborate dissertation by M. Schlesinger, on the introduction to the German translation of the book " Ikkarim," Frankfort, a. M. 1844.

No. 35. This commentary is in the Parisian National Library, fonds de l'orat. No. 111, entitled, פירוש לס' המופת

It appears from the preface that the author wrote it at the request of one of his friends, and took Ibn Roshd as a guide, whom he considered as the most profound commentator of Aristotle, and protected him against some attacks of Levi ben Gerson. It is visible, from the close of the postscript, that he concluded it at Huesca (וואישקה), in the year 1446.

No. 36. At the close of the manuscript of the "Intentio philosophorum," with a commentary of Moses of Narbonne (anc. fonds No. 358), the copyist, Isaac ben Chabib, reports that he concluded it on the 7th of Tebeth, 5232 (December 17, 1471), at Saragossa, the seat of learning of the great scholar and philosopher, teacher and Rabbi, Abraham ben Bibag.

No. 37. Joseph ben Shemtob was an appointed officer at the court of the King of Castilia, but what office he had is unknown to us. He was highly respected and in the presence of the king and high officers he disputed sometimes on philosophical subjects. He relates it in the preface of his commentary on ethics. He was the most fertile Jewish author in Spain, As we find nowhere (compare Wolf, De Rossi) an exact and complete register of his works, I will enumerate them here in a probable chronological order, which shall also comprise among them such which are perhaps not extant any more, but which are quoted by the author himself in such works that are accessible to me.

1st. A small treatise "On domestic affairs" הנהגת הבית composed when he was in his youthful days. Quoted below No. 5.

2d. Commentary on the בחינות עולם "Examination of the world," by Jedaja Bedersi. Quoted Ibid.

3d. Commentary on a work of his father, Shemtob, entitled: ספר היסודות "Book of the fundaments." Quoted Ibidem.

4th. Commentary on the renowned letter, "Be not like your fathers," by Profiat Duran. Quoted further No. 7. This commentary was, according to De Rossi, published in Constantinople, and is also in manuscript in the Parisian National Library.

5th. עין הקירא or "Eye (that is guide) of the preacher." A treatise on the morality and on the art to preach (quoted in No. 7), and is in manuscript (de l'anc. f. No. 158) in the Parisian National Library.

6th. Commentary on "Lamentations of Jeremiah," composed in Medina del Campo, in the year 1444. See De Rossi, Catal. cod. 177.

7th. כבוד אלהים "Glory of God." Treatise on the highest good and the aim of science and knowledge. Published at Ferrara, 1536; composed in the year 1442, thirteen years before he wrote the commentary on "Ethics," as he himself stated in the preface of the latter, on the occasion of the relations of Aristotle's "Ethics" to the moral precepts of the Mosaic law.

8th. Translation of a polemical treatise against the Christians from the Spanish, by Rabbi Chasdai Crescas, entitled: מאמר הנבדל (Cited No. 9.)

9th. Commentary on the treatise "On the material intellect, or on the possibility of uniting with God or attachment to God" אפשרת הדבקות by Ibn Roshd. (Manuscript of the Oratorien fonds No. 136.)

10th. רעת עליון "The knowledge of the Most High," or refutation of a treatise, entitled: סוד הגמ'ל ("The secret of retribution)," on fatalism, by the Apostate Abner, and the views as they were expressed by Rabbi Chasdai. (Cited many times in No. 13.)

11th. Commentary on the Aristotlean treatise, "On the soul."

12th. Commentary on the treatise, "On the Intellectum" מאמר השכל by Alexander Aphrodisi, or rather on an extract of it composed by Ibn Roshd (cited Ibid. 1, 6 and 10). The manuscript of this commentary, which was concluded on the Feast of Booths, 5215 (Oct., 1454), at Segovia, was purchased lately by the Parisian National Library.

13th. מ"ס" המדות A very complete commentary "On Ethics to Nikomachus." This most important work of our author was composed by him during the time of 100 days, and was concluded on the first of Nissan, 5215 A. M. (March 20, 1451), There are in the Parisian National Library two manuscripts of it. Manusc. fonds No. 308; Orat. No. 121.

No. 38. The manuscript, No. 107 fonds de l'orat., contains three works by Shemtob, viz: המאמר בסבה התכליתית or treatise "On the final cause of creation," a treatise "On the primitive matter and its relations to the form, according to the views of ancient philosophers, and especially those of Aristotle and his interpreters," was probably composed in Segovia in 1461; furthermore, כאור כח הרברי "Explanation of speech," or "Capability for reason," or commentary on a part of the treatise "On the soul," by Aristotle (I. iii. c. 4–7), was concluded at Almazan on the first of Marcheshwan, 5241 A. M. (Sept. 28, 1478).

The manuscript, No. 329 anc. f., contains the commentary on the "Physics," by Aristotle, was concluded at Almazan on the second of Marcheshwan, 5241 A. M. (Oct. 6, 1480.) The commentary on the "Moreh," by Maimonides, was printed.

No. 39. Compare, concerning Elia del Medigo, Geiger in Melo Chofnaim, S. xxiv., xxv. and xxii. The treatise "On the intellectum," is without any title in the Hebrew manuscript in the Parisian National Library, No. 328 anc. f. It is identical with that of Joseph del Medigo, with the words: "Profound question on the unity of intellectus" (שכל היוליאני), Geiger ib. heb. text p. 17. Elia concluded this treatise about the end of Shebat, 5242 (January, 1482).

The same manuscript contains also his commentary on the treatise, בעצם הגרגל ("De substantia orbis"), concluded at Bassano on the 5th of Marcheshwan, 5246 A. M. (Oct. 14, 1485.) Both works were composed by the inducement of Joh. Pico of Mirandola, and also the Latin commentary on the "Physics," by Aristotle. It is among the Latin manuscripts of the Parisian National Library, No. 6508, where are also added some letters which our Elia wrote with his own hand to Pico de Mirandola.

The "Bechinath hadath," published in Basel, 1629, was republished, with an excellent commentary, by J. Reggio, Wien, 1833.